Acknowledgment :
Farmer Sidney Greenland

First published 1978

Originated by
J. M. Dent & Sons Ltd
Printed in Great Britain

I Am a Farmer

Photographs : Dick Swayne
Production : Peter Savage
Art Direction : Keith Naris
Words : Val Williams

J.B. Lippincott Company
Philadelphia and New York

I am a farmer. My name is Sue.

“Mucking out” the milking shed is
very hard work.
The cows are patiently waiting
as I walk in with their breakfast.

This is the big
bucket of feed.

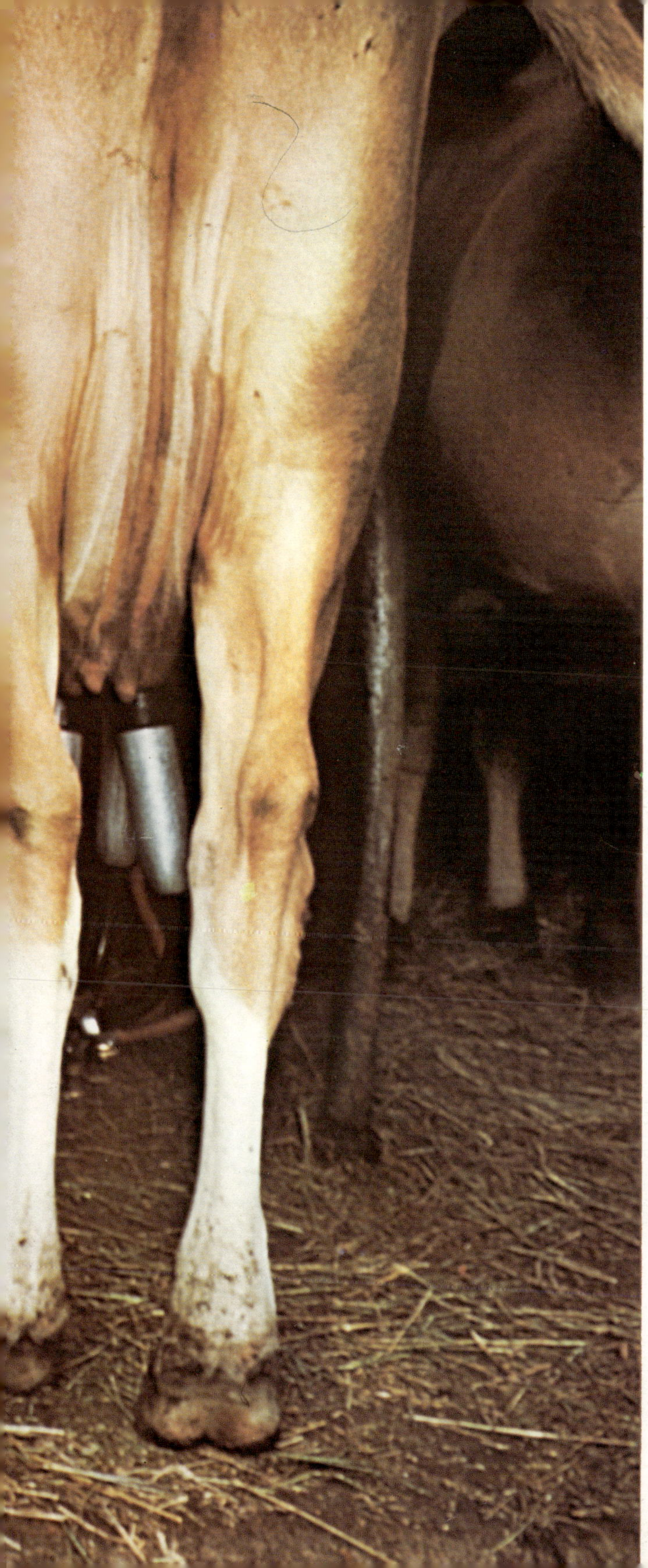

Gently,
I put on the
milking
machine.
The milk is
soon flowing
– white
and fresh.
Every cow
gives pints
and pints.
That is my
special cow,
Judy, looking
at me.

At last it's time for breakfast.
While I eat my eggs and bacon,
I think about my friends on the farm.

Here's Judy,
Dick the rooster,
Charka the donkey,
and Fred the farmhand.

Feeding time
seems never
to stop.
I like to
watch the
calves stick
their noses
deep into the
feed bucket.
They are
always
hungry!

What a clucking and squawking! It's breakfast time for the chickens. Peck, peck, peck go their busy, bobbing heads, snapping up the chicken feed as fast as I can pour it out.

This is the tractor that Fred will drive out to the fields. Today we start haymaking.

Fred swings the hay up to me. Standing on top of the hay wagon, I can almost touch the sky!

Both Fred and I look forward
to a break for lunch.

The hay has to be stored in the barn for the winter.

Time to
collect the
eggs. We'll
take most of
them to
market
to be sold,
but we always
keep
enough for
ourselves.
Everyone in
my family
likes nice,
fresh eggs.
I like brown
ones best.

I wave good-bye to the man who drives the milk tanker. He will call at several farms before he's finished today. Charka doesn't like trucks and cars. He stands quietly, nibbling at the green grass, though he trots over when he sees me.

There are always jobs to be done on a farm. A few hard blows and the fence post is mended.

I must not forget to pick an apple or two for the animals I'm off to visit now.

The pigs can smell the apples in my pocket.

Aren't they fine,
fat porkers!

Now it's time to go home. What a busy day I've had on the farm!

U.S. Library of Congress Cataloging in Publication Data
Swayne, Dick.
I am a farmer.
SUMMARY: Farmer Sue describes some of the chores, animals, and helpers on her farm.
1. Agriculture—Juvenile literature. 2. Farmers—Juvenile literature. 3. Farm life—Juvenile literature.
[1. Farmers. 2. Farm life. 3. Occupations]
I. Title.
S519.S898 1978 630 77-10758
ISBN-0-397-31776-X
ISBN-0-397-31795-6 (pbk.)